A JUNGIAN PRIMER:
GUIDE TO DEVELOPMENTAL SPIRITUAL CONSCIOUSNESS
THEORY AND GERONTOLOGICAL PRACTICE

by

Thomas Pastorello, Ph.D.
Professor Emeritus, 2002
Syracuse University
College of Human Services and Health Professions

Contents Outline

A JUNGIAN PRIMER

INTRODUCTION

Archetypes

Cultural Context

A JUNGIAN PSYCHOLOGY OF SELF:

STATICS AND DYNAMICS

The Biology of Consciousness and Unconsciousness

Time Non-transcendent

Unconsciousness: Statics

    Shadow, Anima(us) and Persona

    Ego

The Psychology of Consciousness and Unconsciousness:

Dynamics

    Individuation as a Dialectic Process

    Self as Emergent from Relationships

PRAXIS

Introduction

- The Structures and Procedures of Dream Analysis
  - Introduction
  - Structure
  - Structural Transformation
  - Dream Analysis Procedures
  - Generalized Analysis Procedures
- SPIRITUALITY
- Synchronicity
  - Introduction
  - Time Transcendent
  - Implications of Time Transcendent:
  - for Spirituality and Synchronicity
- Dreams of Prophesy
- A Working Definition of Spirituality
  - Spirituality-based Practice
  - Personal Transformation
  - Spiritual Community
- REFERENCES
- DEDICATION

Diagrammatic Outline

Personality Development "Mandala" Model: Individuation (Jung/Pastorello)

(driven by Coniunctio Archetype)

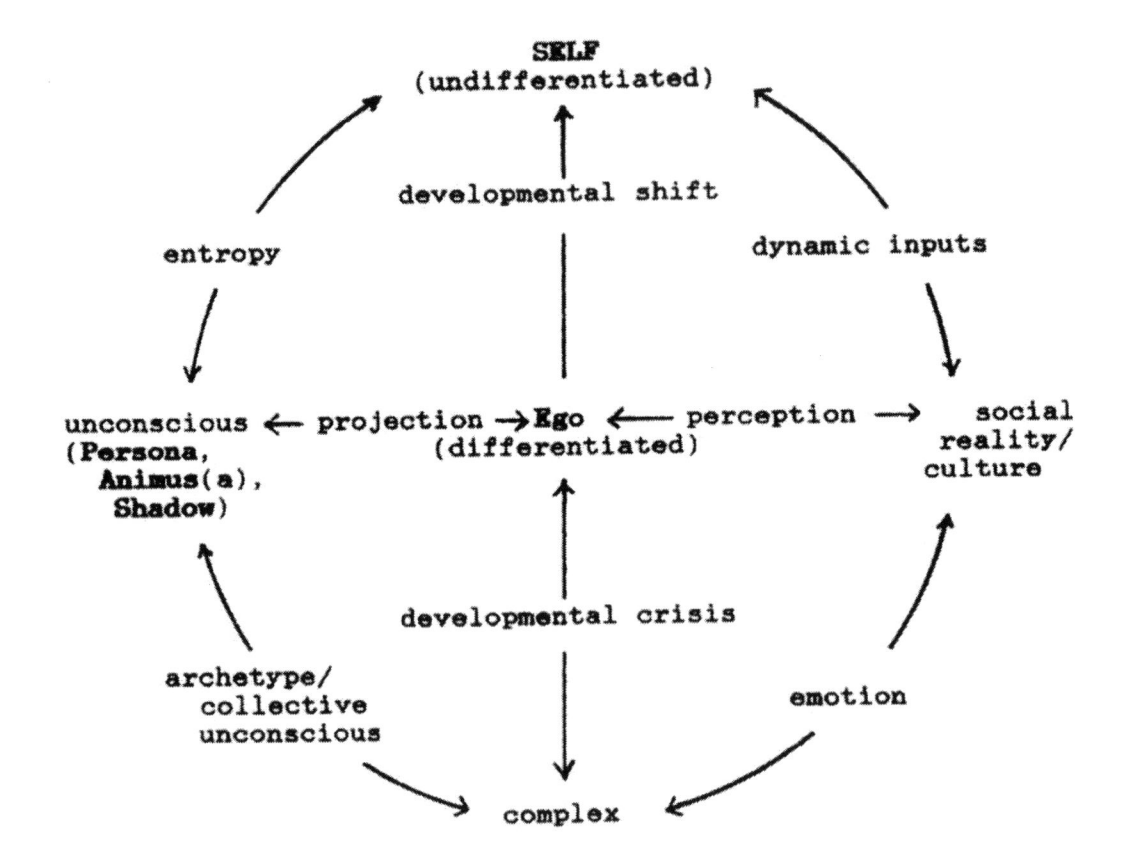

SELF
(undifferentiated)

developmental shift

entropy — dynamic inputs

unconscious ← projection → **Ego** ← perception → social reality/culture
(**Persona**, (differentiated)
Animus(a),
Shadow)

developmental crisis

archetype/collective unconscious — emotion

complex

INTRODUCTION

Spiritual development is that life-long -- and, perhaps, transcendental – process which moves the individual to spiritual consciousness. As an orientation to life and death, spiritual consciousness is characterized by the search for meaning transcendent of socially constructed reality. An understanding of the dynamics of spiritual development and spiritual consciousness is approached from a Jungian perspective; consequently, this treatise opens with an overview of Jungian concepts, the theoretical structures which define relationships among the concepts and, as one application of the theoretical structures, principles of dream analysis. The treatise closes with broader implications for a practice which fosters development of spiritual consciousness.

The recent publication of <u>The Red Book</u> of C.G. Jung (2009) gives documentation of Jung's spiritual developmental journey from 1914 to 1930, in terms of his mandala art and dream interpretations. This primer serves also to make comprehensible to the lay reader the developmental theory underlying his journal.

Archetypes

The primary example of an archetype of form is the circle. Most generally conceived, an archetype is an innate mental structure for organizing our perceptions, experiences, memories and dreams into universal form, plot and character. The organizing process is rooted in biology. Culture overlays the process and gives content to form as symbol, plot as myth and character as Self. The process is developmental. Society, in its many forces and to various degrees, hinders and facilitates wholistic development. Archetype, therefore, is the elemental structure and dynamic of individual and social life and growth, and as such is central to theory which attempts to integrate metaphysical knowledge and applications from biology to physics and a comprehensive range of behavioral and social science research. Underlying transformation in spiritual consciousness is archetypal transformation.

Before examining the specifics of archetypal processes as we will employ them, it may be helpful to note, for purposes of analogy, a concept from Chomskian linguistics: the human's innate capacity for language. Noam Chomsky does not argue that we are born knowing language. We are born, however, with the capacity to structure learned vocabulary into nouns, verbs and objects grammatically (Robertson, 1995). What accounts for speech in the human, relative to other upper primates, is not the larynx but rather the mental structure which allows an innate understanding of grammatical language (Pinker, 1994). Chimpanzees, including the celebrated "Nim Chimpsky" have learned linguistic expression by means of computer operation but, within that expression, do not seem to experience any sense that something is wrong with their tendency to string together nouns as a complete "sentences," nor to use nouns and objects in a sentence without the appearance of a transitive or intransitive verb (Bickerton, 1990). Human toddlers forming even their first sentences not only avoid such tendencies, they resist mentally the misguided attempts of some adults teach grammatically inappropriate "baby talk." As we examine archetypal processes, it will be argued, in parallel fashion to Chomskian theory, not that we humans are born knowing symbol, myth and Self; rather, that we are born with the innate capacity to structure experience and learned meanings into universal forms of symbol, myth and Self.

In its specifics, archetype can be understood first as an organizing principle of experience. To live is to be inundated with a chaos of sensory experiences. Form, plot and character are not external aspects of reality. They are the structures we impose on reality. An array of food pellets on the ground, each roughly equidistant from a central point, is to a cat an array of food pellets. To a human, the array of pellets is an array of pellets -- and a circle. We select out the extraneous noise of experience by organizing sensory input into meaningless scatter and meaningful pattern. The organizing patterns of mind universal to all within the human family are archetypal. Archetype is meaningful pattern.

Cultural Context

The universal availability of circle makes it particularly amenable to cultural overlay. Great places of spirituality and worship are circular – from Stonehenge to Delphi's Temple of Athena to the domed caverns of the Anasazi Indians to the Duomos of Catholic Italy. Not surprisingly then, the circle is a cross-cultural symbol of Self-wholeness, finding common expression in cultural symbols as diverse as the mandala of the Tibetans (Cornell, 1994) and the medicine wheel of the Hopi and other indigenous peoples of the Americas (Bopp, 1989). Jung reports (1989a) that at one time in his life he sketched a mandala in The Red Book every morning, and of this he said: "only gradually did I discover what the mandala really is: 'Formation, Transformation, Eternal Mind's eternal recreations.' And that is the self..." (pp.195-196). The leap in understanding from circle as meaningful organization to the mandala as symbol of self is best explicated in terms of processes of archetypal formation.

In our memory and in our reflections the details of experience are not recounted. We do not relive the minutia of life. On the contrary, in our memory and reflection we simplify, summarize and structure experience by projecting patterns of plot. Archetypal plot is meaningful organization of experience into story line. There are just so many plots and just so many myths. And myth is universal. Creation myths, for example, even in their spontaneous and independent development in geographically dispersed cultures, contain a common core of plot (Campbell, 1976). The universality of myth and its transpersonal nature allows its use in psychotherapeutic healing. To know the myth which archetypally guides one's behavior is to know what to change in the "script" that predicts self-destructive behavior (Coleman, 1988). This latter application of archetypal plot is to be discussed as an element of individuation and growth to wholeness.

Who am I? Am I the sum total of my attributes of body and behavior? Am I simply the conscious knower who reflects on Self by recounting everything I ever did or said or witnessed? Who are you? Do I know you only as a chaos of movements in space and time? I am the pattern which society labels character and are you another character in the plot I call my life?

Archetypal character is meaningful organization of experiences with reference Self and other and, as is the nature of archetype, is universal. The dramaturgical metaphor, in its expression of aspects of Self and other, finds a variety of cultural forms from use of the mask in celebration to the scripting of role in theatrical play. Do we see in these cultural manifestations a universal recognition of persona as one aspect of self? How many character expressions may self-contain? Is self the whole which is not the sum of the character parts yet emergent from constituent, internalized characters? Character metaphors are the archetypes within.

Answers to these questions start from self-insight. Consequently, it is to a psychology of self-insight that we now turn. Paradoxically, the more we delve into the inner Self, the more of an outward direction our journey will take. Our journey now is from Self, to its expression in mandala and wheel, to its creation and re-creation of our mythic life story of ultimate spiritual fulfillment and wholeness.

JUNGIAN PSYCHOLOGY OF SELF: STATICS AND DYNAMICS

The Biology of Consciousness and Unconsciousness

Jungian psychology is best known in its popular manifestation as the personality theory of functional types and introverted and extroverted attitude. Our discussion of Self cannot begin here. Personality theory lies around the periphery of the circle of Self – it represents only the conscious self. To delve within, we need to examine the unconscious self. To allow a scientifically meaningful connection to quartered mandala and quartered medicine wheel, we need also to examine the structure of the brain. An understanding of the unconscious, as that of the archetype, begins with biology. What relevant knowledge do we have of the biology of consciousness and of the unconscious?

Experimental research involving brain surgery and epilepsy yields observations of interest (Penrose, 1989). One form of surgical intervention for epilepsy completely severs the corpus callosum, which divides the two hemispheres of the cerebrum – the large convoluted portion of the brain. The two sides of the cerebrum are often described relative to one another in terms of their division of capabilities. For example, the right side of the cerebrum is described as capable of geometrical thinking. Verbal abilities are centered on the left. These types of functions are best described as "centered," rather than isolated, on either side because multifunctional capabilities permeate the entire brain and the corpus callosum allows cross-hemisphere communication.

One form of experimentation with split-brain patients is structured as follows. An individual is shown different stimuli to different eyes. A pencil is shown to the right eye where, given the cross-wiring of the sense organs and the brain, it registers in the left portion of the cerebrum. The left side houses the speech center, including Broca's Area where sentences are formulated (as well as Wernicke's Area where language is comprehended). A cup is shown to the left eye. It registers in the right cerebrum, surgically segregated from access to the speech center, but with tactile capabilities within its sphere. When the individual in this experiment must indicate whether the pencil or the cup was perceived, he seems to respond at two distinct levels of consciousness! When verbally addressed, i.e., asked what object he saw, he says "pencil." When blindfolded and instructed to feel the two objects in front of him (pencil and cup) and pick up the object he saw, he picks up the cup. The individual feels no sense of dissonance about the seemingly contradictory choices. He is of two consciousnesses and, at the same time, of one consciousness – two parts and one dialectic unity.

In a parallel experiment, when a young man has whispered into his left ear (right brain –more emotional, less analytical) "What do you wish to be?" – his answer is "racing car driver". The process repeated for his right ear (and left brain) yields the response of "draftsman". We witness two aspects of his Self, distinct yet unitary. At any one time, one aspect of Self-expression may be active in one sphere of consciousness and another in a different sphere. At the same moment, one aspect may be in consciousness, the other actively in unconsciousness. Consciousness does not express true Self, nor does unconsciousness. Self is emergent from the dialectic tension between conscious and unconscious forces.

Logically, as we move from this biological research to psychological concerns, we are only steps from a fuller understanding of Jung's four-part division of consciousness and unconsciousness -- Ego, Persona Shadow and Anima(us) -- into the unity of Self. That information may be actively in unconsciousness, i.e., dialectically integrated with and influential to consciousness, is suggested by a study which demonstrates that experimental subjects can "learn" to predict where an "X" will next appear on a computer screen even though complex simultaneous equations, not consciously known by the subject, underlie the seemingly random pattern of "X" appearances (Coleman, 1992). "Blind sight" studies (Blakeslee, 1991) reinforce the notion that information, active only in the unconscious, may be influential to the consciousness. In some individuals with healthy, functional eyes a limitation in field of vision is caused by brain damage within the visual cortex. In the "blind-sight" studies subjects are asked to describe the object being held in their blind spots. Subjects are at first unable to respond. However, when subjects are asked to relax and guess, some studies show a guess rate of 100% accuracy! Their retinas are healthy and continue to register images in an undamaged region of the brain's lower temporal lobe. The images bypass conscious perception, yet they remain available as usable information.

We witness in these studies the unconscious at work. But where is the unconscious? Some experimental studies suggest that we may better locate the unconscious in time than space. A brief review of this research will set the stage for the presentation of a crucial aspect of unconsciousness – the temporal. Understanding unconsciousness as a temporal phenomenon will be the basis for an explication of the key Jungian concepts of collective unconsciousness and synchronicity. The question becomes, therefore, not "Where is the unconscious?" but "When is the unconscious?"

Time Non-transcendent

The key to consciousness may be in the signaling rhythm of the brain's neuron networks and, therefore, the structuring influence of the archetypes of the unconscious may occur during oscillations of consciousness. Research by neuroscientists on the illusory nature of the "stream" of consciousness clarifies the meaning and import of this statement (Blakeslee, 1992a).

Do not think of your grandmother. Now that you have thought of your grandmother, can you explain from where and how you conjured up her image? Neuroscientific research has rejected the notion of a "grandmother cell" (as colloquially put). In spite of the fact that the brain houses a network of 100 billion neurons, we do not have a number of memory storage cells sufficient to contain and retain all of the images of experience we can evoke. There is not one nerve cell which, when activated, evokes the image (or vicarious experience) of grandmother. It is more likely that the brain maintains nerve cells which, when activated, evoke different aspects of the experience of grandmother, e.g., grayness, slowness, softness, frailty, warmth, etc. The network of cells which produce grandmother in the mind's eye must be fired simultaneously. A conscious awareness of grandmother then is emergent from the neurological process which evokes simultaneously all of the characteristics which mean grandmother. As a mental experience, grandmother is the whole which is greater than the sum of her parts.

If not in any one cell of the brain, where is this emergent image of grandmother? For her image to enter consciousness, all of the cells which mean grandmother must fire at the same time. What is meant by "the same time" can be defined within a precise range: within 50 to 100 milliseconds. All the networked grandmother cells must oscillate within this critical frequency for her image to emerge. This neuroscientific perspective views consciousness, therefore, as a sequence of oscillating networks and not as a continuous stream. Consciousness forms and falls away every 50 to 100 milliseconds. Consciousness is the illusion of continuity, much as a movie is truly a set of still images rapidly presented to create the effect of real motion and continuity. Consequently, the question becomes not where is conscious imagery but when is it.

If consciousness is every 50 to 100 milliseconds, then is unconsciousness when nerve cells are not in oscillation? Is it during periods of non-neuro-oscillation that archetypal structure is projected to give form to sensory input? Are neural networks patterns determined by archetypes? Are neural network patterns in effect the archetypes of the unconscious and, if so, does neuro-oscillation theory explain human universalities in archetypal projections? Can archetypal universals of form, symbol, character and Self be located in the brain, and if so, what may be the consequences of this understanding for the spacial and temporal analysis of archetypal content in dreams and artistic output? At this stage of research, the answers to these questions are speculative. Nevertheless, speculative answers can be organized within a coherent theory. The quadrant mandala theory of dream and art archetypal analysis to be developed in this work, provides an explanatory theory (for practice application). A full presentation of that theory must be preceded by conceptual clarification relative to Jung's notions of unconscious formation and projection of Self-character archetypes. The Psychology of Consciousness and

Unconsciousness: Statics

Jung's dynamic conceptualization of processes of unconscious projection and conscious perception are central to his understanding of personality structure, and entail the incorporation of the concepts of complex, attitude, functional types, Ego, Persona, Anima(us) and Shadow, differentiation, individuation, coniunctionis and Self. A review of these concepts will allow for an explication of quadrant mandala analysis theory, and related notions of collective unconscious, time-transcendent and transcendence.

Archetypal structure of the unconscious (Shadow, Anima, Persona, complex) will begin this discussion. It is to be followed by the more popularly known Jungian personality structure of the conscious mind (Ego, attitude and function). The dynamics which connect these minds into a dialectic whole (differentiation, individuation and coniunctionis) conclude this discussion.

Shadow, Anima(us) and Persona. -- The character archetypes organize self-referent experiences and form the basis for an emergent sense of the Self. The individuation process by which this occurs, however, is complex. It is also dialectic and, consequently, necessarily preceded by differentiation of the splinter selves: Shadow, Anima(us) and Persona. Sense of Self emerges simultaneously with the formation of splinter selves, is fluid, dynamic, continuous and ever-changing as different aspects of the splinter selves partially enter and partially withdraw from consciousness.

The Self has long been recognized as being shaped by social forces. James' distinction between the I of the Self and the Me of the Self is a distinction between the conscious knower and the attributes of Self which are socially recognized and labeled (Gergen, 1971). James' theory, however, is one of consciousness. Jung asks us to consider how children deal with social disapproval of Self as they are reared – in particular, social disapproval of our poorly controlled animal-based expressions. When instinct is aggressive and social reaction repressive, how do we make Self-sense of our behavior? When instinct is gluttonous and social reaction demands moderation; or when defecation is performed publicly on biological imperative and social reaction disapproving and firm, how do we make Self-sense out of these behaviors?

Since such Self behaviors are not allowed overt expression, they are repressed. Eventually, they no longer remain part of conscious awareness of Self and adhere to the unconscious archetypal pattern which allows them form. Denied expression, unconscious form grows strong. Denied unconscious expression over significant developmental periods of time, form becomes splinter self. Form becomes Shadow. The darker side to self is Shadow. The term "darker" is not to be given pejorative connotations. Shadow is a true aspect of Self, but one not allowed social light. The "dark" side of the Yin-Yang is a true aspect of its wholeness, but different from its integral other half in its being on the shaded side of the mountain. Nevertheless, because of social pressures, the Shadow is seldom allowed overt expression and, therefore, moderate or positive expression.

"Shadow" is clearly a better term for describing this type of splinter self than "dark side." The latter term too readily suggests dichotomy; the former term is more clearly dialectic. Darkness can exist without light, as it does in the inner recesses of a cave. A shadow necessarily exists only with light. Only light allows the casting of shadow. Light is defined by its relationship to shadow; shadow by its relationship to light. Light and shadow are in dialectic relationship.

Too often, in the unindividuated, the Shadow's expression is by means of projection. The tendencies which we deny as part of ourselves we project onto others. The tendencies which we cannot consciously accept in ourselves we see as attributes of others. It is they who are aggressive, gluttonous, out of control. Unconscious Shadow projection, therefore, can be the basis for racism, sexism, homophobia, ageism and handicapism. Conscious acceptance and ownership of the Shadow, on the other hand, can be the basis for genuine and meaningful inter-personal relationships and personal wholeness (Stevens, 1991). The shadow is a moral problem. Jung has argued that conscious integration of the shadow can proceed only with considerable moral effort (Aziz, 1990). The development of this moral potentiality is to be explicated and explored in both the theory and practice sections of this work. First, however, splinter selves other than the Shadow need be defined.

In the total gender identity consciousness of the child, where do socially disapproved displays of feminine behaviors for the boy and masculine behaviors for the girl adhere in the unconscious? For the boy, the archetypal splinter self-structure is labeled by Jung the Anima; and for the girl, the Animus. In the man and the woman, these contrasexual splinter selves continue their existence with varying degrees of developmental conscious expression and unconscious projection. The wholistic man is alienated from his feminine self by virtue of social pressures to gender conformity. The wholistic woman is similarly repressed. The theory of splinter self-projection, outlined above relative to the Shadow, applies in relation to the Anima and Animus too. He discovers his feminine side by projection of Anima on a suitable other. She discovers her masculine side by projection of Animus on a suitable other. The process is called love.

Love is not to be confused with individuation. As is to be explicated later in the theory section of this work, love as unconscious projection of contrasexual splinter self is only the first step in an individuation process which must actively involve conscious processes. At the unconscious stage of projection, however, what is love? The heterosexual man-woman love relationship is given emphasis in the Jungian concept of the "marriage quarternio". The scheme is heuristic and readily extended to the homosexual love relationship. In the case of man-woman relationships, the first possible type is the simple uncomplicated personal relationship as, for example, between colleagues at work, next door neighbors or between sales clerks and customers. Man and woman relate to each other consciously.

In the case where man relates to woman by means of his projection of his Anima onto her, or woman relates to man by means of her projection of her Animus onto him, we have the second of four possible relationships in the quarternio . This second type is strongly rooted in the unconscious mind and may be described colloquially as "love at first sight." He is not in love with the real woman, but rather with his projection onto her of his ideal woman. In effect, he has fallen in love with himself. Likewise, in this type of relationship, the woman who projects her Animus has fallen in love with that aspect of herself that she has been out of touch with in a gender conformist society: her masculine self. If the Anima(us) projection continues to deny the reality of the other person, the relationship is doomed to failure. Disillusionment readily sets in as the reality of the other person forces itself into a relationship unprepared for it.

On the other hand, the relationship may grow into "true love," i.e., the third type, if reality and unconscious compensatory needs are developed in relation to one another. In this case the relationship progresses to the point where he allows her masculine side free expression and she allows his feminine side free expression. They are secure with each other enough to be comfortable with self-expressions not allowed in gender conformist social settings. With her, he can cry; with him she can be assertive. A love relationship of this third type of the quarternio contributes to the growth and individuation of each person as each gains greater sight in to his or self-unconscious splinter selves and each makes the insights a greater element of conscious awareness. She is no longer solely his Anima projection because in their relationship, she has allowed his direct expression of Anima. He is no longer solely her Animus projection because in their relationship, he has allowed her direct expression of Animus.

In the fourth aspect of the quaternio set of relationships, Animus relates directly to Anima. The couple is One and whole with the collective unconscious. With the fourth type of relationship, one has found one's soul mate. Love now is unconditional, i.e., not contingent upon the partners roles, achievements, possessions or successes in the larger social world. One is loved for one's true Self, not one's Persona. Each person in the relationship is free to give expression to Shadow as well as Anima(us). This ultimate love relationship in the quarternio set is soul to soul. The Latin word for soul is, in fact, Anima. Regardless of sexual orientation or gender, central to the development of wholeness is the expression of Anima. Hill (1992) has argued that developmental wholeness moves from a static femininity to a dynamic femininity for both sexes. The very goal of analysis, according to Hillman (1972) is the acceptance of femininity.

An adaptation of the quarternio scheme to homosexual relationship can be made with minimal modification. Gender conformity and sexual orientation are different issues. Homosexuals experience the same gender conformity pressures as do heterosexuals. Therefore, gay men develop Anima splinter selves and lesbians develop Animus splinter selves. Their sexual orientation, however, makes a person of the same sex the recipient of their contrasexual self-projections in a type two and three quaternio relationship. Projection onto a same-sex other is the only modification required for the homosexual quaternio scheme. Contrasexual projection onto a same-sex individual is not a contradiction in terms if every individual is viewed from the Jungian perspective as a dialectic composite of masculine and feminine. The type four, "soul mate" relationship, also involves unconditional love and a fusion of unconscious archetypes in a sense of collective unconscious Oneness. Of course, as with the heterosexual quaternio, The most superficial type of relationship is from Persona to Persona. What needs to be addressed at this point, for a rounding out of this discussion of the splinter selves, is Persona.

The Latin word for mask is Persona. The process of socialization, of becoming a member of society, can be visualized as one of acquiring social masks. Each role the individual is assigned is accompanied by a mask. To become a mother, a social worker, a bowler, etc., is to acquire masks to wear socially during role performance. Behaviors which do not fall into the organization of the Shadow, most often find conscious expression through the mask.

Persona is not to be confused with Ego. Jung (1971) describes Ego as the empirical personality; Persona is an archetype of the unconscious. People do not typically see themselves as performing socially in dramaturgical terms. Shakespeare notwithstanding, individuals do not see themselves as mere actors upon a stage. They invest themselves in their social roles. Roles are not scripts for them, they are identities. What is lost consciously is the sense that we are more than the roles we play. Self is greater than the sum of its social parts.

Consider the following exercise. Stand in front of a mirror. Ask yourself who you are. If you are like most people, you'll list all of your social masks, e.g., "I am a mother, a social worker, a bowler..." Now take off one of your masks, e.g., your parent mask, and ask yourself again who you are. You offer the list of identities again -- this time with one mask missing. Take off another mask. Ask yourself again who you are. Continue the process. What do you say when you remove the last mask? Who are you then? If at this existential moment you are no one, you have experienced a Persona-related crisis. You are forced to acknowledge the existence of a true Self and the need to get to know it. Later, in this work and in another context, the persona-crisis will be re-interpreted as a spiritual crisis and getting to know Self, outside of the context of socially constructed reality, will be presented as a crucial practice related aspect of spiritual development.

What then is Persona? It is the unconscious archetype which hides from consciousness the mask-like nature of our social identities. Persona is the archetype which organizes our social role cognitions, expectations, attitudes, affects and behavioral activities and, by means of projection, makes the play of life seem real. Persona projects out the social mask by allowing ourselves to view others only through the eye holes of our masks. Others are assigned their roles in consonance with our Persona character. In failing to see true Self, we fail to see true other. Other is reduced to an actor, her or his ascribed characteristics, including the superficialities of skin color and genital structure, become more important than innate qualities. Relationships to others viewed only through our masks are inauthentic.

Getting in touch with true Self involves allowing the masks -- ours and others' -- to slip in authentic relationships. Again, significant others guide the recognition of Self. For example, to have a mentor is to be guided socially by someone who is experienced in the ways of the social world. To admire a mentor is to grow socially. To see the mentor as a real person with flaws, and not as an idealized masked figure, is to grow in terms of Self. The truly good mentor is not perfect. In performing her or his role well, the mentor allows social growth; in allowing her or his imperfections to be recognized, the mentor allows growth of Self. If minimizing Shadow projection and Anima(us) projection is to allow truer knowledge of Self, then to minimize Persona projection is also to allow truer knowledge of Self.

Wholeness is defined by Jung as becoming true Self. Wholeness is the culmination of the process of individuation. And individuation is that which allows full integration of unconscious splinter selves into consciousness. Therefore, prior to any discussion of dynamics, must come some closure on statics, i.e., as the structure of unconsciousness has been delineated, the structure of the conscious mind must now be explicated.

Ego. -- The archetype of the conscious mind is Ego. Jungian-based psychology in the popular literature has emphasized Jung's classificatory system of personality. It may serve as the operational definition of Ego statics. Unfortunately, the popular literature misses Jung's main point, as to the role Ego plays in individuation dynamics. In this work, Ego statics are described as a necessary prelude to the theory of individuation dynamics.

If the job of the unconscious is to structure perception in accordance with archetypal forms, including those of the three splinter selves, the job of Ego is to provide the perceptions. It is the Ego archetype which is most in touch with environmental reality and allows perceptions of the outer world. The static structure of Ego consists of two attitudes and four functional types.

The two attitudes are the labeled by the well-known descriptors of introversion and extraversion. If the former perceptual orientation is represented by the mystical, the symbolic, the striving to understand and to know Self; the latter is represented by the practical, the concrete, the striving to communicate and to know other. In terms of philosophical personality, the introvert has been described as Platonic, and the extravert as Aristotelian. Although this latter distinction may suffice in a discussion of statics, no personified pairing better defines Ego attitudinal structure than Nietzche's use of the mythic figures of Dionysus and Apollo (1954). For Nietzche, as for Jung, the pairing is dialectic. The purpose of this mythic pairing is not contrast but exercise in the dialectic discipline of knowing two perceived "opposites" as inextricable facets of one reality. This point needs to be emphasized, and these mythic metaphors need to be elaborated upon, as our topic moves from statics to dynamics.

Jung's Ego-based classificatory system of personality further structures each attitude into four functional types: Thinking, feeling, sensation and intuition -- each of which provides its own mode of perception of the possibilities inherent in a situation. Thinking and feeling are rational functions, in that they filter perception. Ego provides not the direct perceptions, but the analyzed perceptions of the thinking type or the judged perceptions of the feeling type. Ego is of the thinking or feeling functional type, not both. Sensation and intuition are irrational functions, in that they provide perceptions directly. The sensation type takes in all details directly; the intuitive type takes in the situation as a whole, in terms of its perceived mood-tone. Ego is of the sensate or intuitive functional type, but not both.

Ego is characterized by a dominant function, rational or irrational (Thinking = T, Feeling = F, Sensate = S, Intuitive = I) and a minor function (thinking = t, feeling = f, sensate = s, intuitive = i). The minor function is rational if the dominant one is irrational and irrational if the dominant one is rational. Sixteen Personality Types are thereby generated: Introverted Ts, Ti, Fs, Fi, St, Sf, It, If and Extraverted Ts, Ti, Fs, Fi, St, Sf, It and If. In order to understand individuation dynamics; however, it is important to note that, in effect, one should conceive of thirty-two Personality Types. Each conscious personality type has its corresponding dialectic opposite in the unconscious. The Jungian unconscious is compensatory. If, for example, the individual manifests as Introverted Ti, then the individual's unconscious may be characterized, in compensatory fashion, as Extraverted Fs. Within Jung's depth psychology, one learns of one's manifest personality type not for the purpose of solidifying one's identity, but for the purpose of learning the direction one' personality development should take for wholistic Self-development. At any one moment, personality is the fluid expression of the temporal dialectic link between unconscious and conscious functions.

No one is of a pure personality type. Personality exists along a continuum from introverted to extraverted, from thinking to feeling, etc. Personality is not a frozen snap-shot of a point on this continuum. It is a movie of dynamic movement along the continuum. This analogy fails, however, to the extent that it falsely suggests personality development to be linear. The nature of individuation dynamics, of which personality development is a small part, is dialectic. It is to a discussion of dialectical individuation dynamics, therefore, that this work must now turn.

The Psychology of Consciousness and Unconsciousness: Dynamics

Individuation as a Dialectic Process. -- Imagine the personal unconscious as a sphere encompassing the archetypes of Shadow, Anima(us) and Persona. Imagine a sphere of consciousness representing Ego. The spheres are not to be conceived as independent entities in time and space. They touch, overlap and partially merge, like two soap bubbles joining in air. Their merger is not structurally fixed. Their overlap in space is greater at some times and lesser at other times -- but they cannot exist apart, independently of one another. Imagine that geometrical configuration which is the structure of their area of overlap. At the center of that structure is Self. And Self is whole when the two spheres are fully concentric -- when the center of the unconscious, the conscious and the Self are the same point in time and space. Individuation is the centering force of the spherical mergence.

The energy which fuels individuation is *coniunctionis* -- Jung's departure from Freud's limited energy principle of libido and Jung's word for the dialectic merging into one again of the duality and the Maya-like illusions of the reality created by consciousness. Jung (1989b) refers to *mysterium coniunctionis* as "nothing less than a restoration of the original state of the cosmos and the divine unconsciousness of the world." (p.463). Wholeness is developed not by a process of eliminating the unconscious forces of Shadow, Anima(us) and Persona but; rather, by acknowledging them, owning them and assimilating them into consciousness (Smith, 1990). Dialectic unity is not the rejection of one opposite for another, nor the obliteration of both in their unity; it is the deeply felt understanding that opposites coexist without contradiction in a greater unity which is emergent from the sum of its parts -- from the dynamic tension between the parts. The Yin/Yang is a most appropriate symbol of the dialectic unity.

Jungian individuation is necessarily preceded by differentiation. One must come to know the contents of the unconscious -- in a dialectic process each part's independent existence must be appreciated in order to understand its dependence within the greater whole. Differentiation of the unconscious involves conscious recognition of the Shadow, Anima(us) and Persona. Individuation is the life-long (and never completed) process of bringing the sphere of the unconscious into the conscious mind.

Wholeness is dependent upon the direction of the process. Wholeness is not accomplished by the sinking of consciousness into unconsciousness. That goes by names other than individuation. That is Dionysian abandon -- drug or alcohol dependence, psychosis, suicide (Neuman, 1995, p.17). Nor does individuation emphasis mere Apollonian form -- Ego-inflated rational understanding of definitions of Shadow, Anima(us) and Persona. Mythological analysis documents that Dionysus and Apollo are one in their dialectic relationship (Hatab, 1990). Wholeness proceeds on the basis of emotionally cathartic recognition and acceptance of one's own splinter selves as dialectic aspects of one's true Self. Apollo and Dionysus are ever newborn twins who struggle to come to the conscious awareness that they are conjoined. Wholeness emerges from their dialectic relationship.

Self as Emergent from Relationships. -- Our conscious recognition of our unconscious selves emerges from relationships in our social environment. During the differentiation aspect of individuation, Shadow is to be recognized in our relationships with those upon whom we prejudicially cast our racist, ethnocentric, sexist, homophobic, handicapist and ageist projections. Anima(us) is to be recognized in our irrational attractions to others. Persona is to be recognized in our workaholic investments in superficial, socially-constructed social roles and in our blind admiration (more often, envy) of "flawless" mentors. In genuine relationships -- relationships which allow prejudice, false love and inflated sense of social status to diminish, differentiation proceeds to conscious integration of splinter selves into Self, i.e., in relationships, differentiation proceeds dialectically to individuation. Where is Self? It is not *in* the person nor in significant others, but dialectically emergent from the totality of the person's relationships.

PRAXIS

Introduction

Individuation to wholeness is a natural process in that it is guided by unrelenting unconscious forces of *coniunctionis*. Nevertheless, it does not unfold easily and naturally because the process of individuation is corrupted by social forces of conformity to socially constructed realities. Those social realities include forces which alienate genuine relationships from being formed -- forces of classist, racial, sexist, heterosexist, handicapist and ageist prejudice and discrimination. Individuation, therefore, necessarily begins with inwardly-focused, non-conformist Self-insights. Ironically and dialectically, it is the inward journey from which can emerge the outward adventure of social transformation -- social constructionist changes which allow everyone the achievement of her or his full wholeness potential and discovery of Self.

Individuation, then, involves the discipline of micro and macro practice. Like Zen, personal and social transformation is the art of doing. There are many such disciplines. Let us begin on the personal and micro level and travel inwardly to the spacial and temporal landscape of our dreams.

The Structures and Procedures of Dream Analysis

Introduction. -- The dream is not wish fulfillment. Freudian principles of dream analysis have emphasized the dream as wish fulfillment; symbols in dreams as condensations and displacements of emotion-laden images from personal experience; associations as individual and personal-- as opposed to collective and archetypal; the dreamer and the dream as analogous to the author and a book; and dream analysis as an art of interpretation of latent content (Freud, 1965). Jungian principles of dream analysis present the dream as compensatory to the conscious situation; dream symbols as expressions of a complex; associations as archetypal and which require mythological amplifications; the dreamer and the dream as analogous to the author and her or his autobiographical play -- in which all the characters are the author; and dream analysis as translation of the dreamer's current situation of individuation in the quite literal terms of manifest content (Jung, 1989).

Some terms require elaboration. For Jung, the center of the action and the core meaning of the dream is the expression of the complex. The complex is a constellation of psychic elements, including thoughts and feelings, which have crystallized around an emotion-laden sensitive area of experience. Even though the complex is formed in experience, it has an innate as well as an environmental component. The innate component is disposition. The child's experience of the same type and degree of abuse, for example, will not form the same intensity of complex nor the same lasting implications for psychological development in different children. Jung's understanding of complex would imply that more resilient and less resilient abused children differ in temperament. The psychic energy of the complex is entropic. It retards individuation. The dream displays the complex as it exists in the unconscious. It also reveals its workings in everyday life and in doing so, the dream message provides dynamic energy for confronting the complex and, thereby, for continued psychological development.

It follows that Jungian dream analysis would be less a matter of creative interpretation and more a matter of translation. The task is not to place the dreamer's work into the context of the analyst's insights about Freudian theory; the task is to help make the unconscious insights of the dreamer conscious for the dreamer's Ego application in the environment. The issue centers on what insight the unconscious reveals that is compensatory to the dysfunctional ignorance of the Ego. The issue centers not on wish fulfillment. Current research with dream subjects rejects the empirical reality of dreams as wish fulfillment and tends to newer theories of dreams as random electrical signals generated by brain neurons as memory is consolidated during REM sleep (Blakeslee, 1992b).

The biological reductionism of recent dream research would seem to contradict Jungian approaches as well as Freudian. The contradiction is more apparent than real. Researchers deal with the story nature of the dream by simply concluding that the human brain concocts a story to organize and make sense of the random images and other sensory outputs made during dream periods of neural firings. But how are the sensory outputs organized? What are the organizing elements? Jungian theory fills this gap in the empirical dream literature efficiently. Archetypes structure sensory output as well as input. During consolidation, the memory fragments most available for archetypal capture and organization are those which have been most salient to the dreamer during the previous day's conscious activities. The experiences which have been most salient have been those filtered through the Ego by the constellations of the complexes. Dream research with subjects who are undergoing marital separation show that they dream about the surrounding issues of family discord. The dream story, therefore, is plot-formation guided by the archetypes of the unconscious and the personal complexes of the individual.

A distinction has not yet been made between the personal and collective unconscious. Essentially, the concept of personal unconscious has been applied to the texts above. Elaboration on the concept of collective unconscious best awaits discussion of space and transcendent time in Jungian theory and its relationship to synchronistic and prophetic dreams. First, however, a focused discussion of dream structure is required.

Structure. -- The dream is a snapshot of the unconscious -- the view of the Yang consciously denied the Yin. The dream, thereby, is an essential basis for the transformational process of individuated wholeness. Transformation involves structural change in the unconsciousness/consciousness configuration. Again, therefore, an understanding of psychodynamics must begin with psychostatics.

Unlike the snapshot, the unconscious has a three dimensionality as well as a two dimensionality. Its two-dimensional structure is the mandala, as quartered circle. This somewhat startling statement derives from personal, unpublished research involving content analyses of personal, family and student dreams, as well as published case evidence. Singer's case study of Charles (1973), who drew quartered mandalas and mandalas squared internally to get in touch with his shadow following encounters with an ape-man in his dreams, is only one of many case illustrations of the quartered circle as an inferred structure of the unconscious. The link between the mandala and the four-part splinter personality structure of Self is suggested by Jung (1989a) when he defines mandala as, from the Sanskrit, a magic circle represented by symmetrical arrangements of the number four. (p.396) It is also, however, the whole which is greater than the sum of the parts: the cross enclosed in a circle has been described as the union of all unreconciled opposites (von Franz, 1998). As such, the quartered mandala is the metaphorical promise of individuated transformation to wholeness.

Content analysis of personal, family and student dreams shows great consistency in the placement of dream imagery on the stage of the dream theater relative to archetypal meanings. Further, there is uncanny consistency between the archetypal geographical structure indicated by personal research and the great cultural traditions of indigenous peoples, in terms of their interpretations of the meanings of the quartered directions of the Medicine Wheel. The universality of the pattern of archetypal imagery, hypothesized as the major original contribution of this work, will require empirical support from neurological brain centers research to augment the qualitative psychological and anthropological research organized in this report.

The working hypothesis of this work on the spacial structure of dreams, and in general of the unconscious, can be expressed with the following extended dramaturgical analogy. If one where to draw a quartered circle on the floor of a stage and look at it from a bird's eye view, stage front-left would be South West, stage front-right would be South East, stage rear-right would be North East and stage rear-left would be North West. If we were to compare the actors who inhabit these stage areas with the archetypal characters who inhabit the two-dimensional (flat ground) area of dream space; Anima would perform stage front-left (SW); Shadow, stage front-right (SE); Ego, stage rear-right (NE) and Persona, stage rear-left (NW). The dream stage opens to the right-rear (NE) to allow Ego content -- in that Ego is not, as defined, an aspect of the unconscious. The NE does represent, relative to the unconscious, the segway to consciousness and, as content analyses will later be used illustrate, the opening to spiritual space and transcendent time.

A three-dimensional perspective incorporates height and depth. Activity above ground level is consistently associated with processes of individuation. On ground level, the surface play is an acting out of the complex with which the dream is concerned. The contents of the realm below ground level are the forms of the Collective Unconscious.

Of these concepts of three-dimensional structure, only Collective Unconscious has not received some elaboration.

Some physicists have argued the potential existence of a universal consciousness -- of a universe that is self-conscious (Kafatos and Nadeau, 1990). The notion of collective unconscious need not posit the existence of such a high level emergent phenomenon. Fundamentally, and perhaps reductionistically, the collective unconscious may be viewed as that set of personal archetypes which all people of all cultures have in common. It is the core set of archetypes of the unconscious, and as such is transpersonal. This core set of archetypes is that which explains the cultural and mythological commonalties across all peoples, in that culture may be viewed as the projections of the collective unconscious. The individual and the culture mirror one another in the archetypes of the collective unconscious. It has been suggested, for example, that the Ego, Persona, Shadow and Anima of every man are the King, Warrior, Magician and Lover of the collective unconscious, and in that sense individual identity is as transpersonal as it is experiential (Moore and Gillette, 1990).

The Collective Unconscious is timeless. Like all archetypes, core archetypes are inherent in the structure of the human brain and, therefore, exist and make their influence known not merely across all currently existing cultures, but all cultures past, present and future. The work of the Third Century philosopher Plotinus (1991), on matters of beauty, truth, spirit, soul, body, God, good and evil, matter, space and time, consciousness and wholeness, seems to anticipate modern dialectic conceptualizations of these phenomena -- including modern quantum physics! Rather than attribute his insights to a gift of prophesy, one may better argue that all human thinkers tap the same archetypal structures for organizing their thoughts about the nature of reality. In fact, physicist Mansfield (1995), alluding to Jungian theory, has argued that, "the great philosopher-sages, whether

Plato and Plotinus in the West or Buddha and Adi Shankara in India, are only expressing archetypal urges when they speak of transcending human limitations and overcoming the world of opposites..." (p.173)   Collective Unconscious is cultural continuity as well as cultural communality.

Dreams in which the protagonist explores subterranean structures are dreams which allow the dreamer to access transpersonal wisdom, including -- if one has ethnic-sensitive respect for such an interpretation -- ancestor wisdom. Symbols found below the dream's ground level tend to resist exploration by means of Freudian personal association techniques. Personal content analyses of dreams indicates that the meanings of the archetypes of the Collective Unconscious are best amenable to amplification oriented to universal story-plot -- in particular, mythology.

Structural Transformations. -- Jungians prefer to work with sets of dreams rather than a single dream. If a single dream is a snapshot of the dreamer's unconscious structure, showing the degree of differentiation among splinter selves; then a set of dreams is a movie, showing changes in degree of differentiation of the splinter selves over time. Individuation may be defined as the developmental process of growing to wholeness as splinter selves are confronted, owned and dialectically incorporated into consciousness. In the more individuated person, the structure of the unconscious should show greater de-differentiation of splinter selves and more nearly the snapshot of the unified Self. Consequently, a set of dreams may show one's pattern of individuation -- progress or lack thereof. A given pattern of individuation may be correlated with changes over time in the dream sets' expressions of the complex and problem-solving messages. Analysis of a set of dreams; therefore, can provide crucial information to facilitate the transformation of individuation.

At this point of the conceptual discussion, a personal illustrative dream may best express metaphorically the individuation-based transformational nature of the workings of the unconscious. The landscape of the dream is a familiar one, visited once before by air in a balloon from a dream past. This landscape is best viewed from the perspective of a balloon. A farmland is covered in snow. Nevertheless, spring flowers burst forth in the SW, in a gentle curvature from the West to the South. A set of objects also defines a curved boarder in the SE, from South to East -- they are ash cans. Trees boarder the NW, curving up from West to North. A farmhouse dominates the NE. Behind it looms a silo. From the farmhouse chimney, smoke rises and encompasses the NE quadrant of the dreamscape in an umbrella-shaped cloud. There is a road below. A car approaches the snowscape from the West. A decision has to be made by the protagonist of the dream in the car. Should he turn left from the road and enter the driveway which leads to the center of the farmhouse land? He does so and then changes his mind. This house is not to be entered again. He makes a broken-U-turn out of the driveway and heads back in the direction of the West. Before the snowscape is lost from his vision, he looks up and to the right into his rear-view mirror and notices the figure made on the driveway by his tire marks in the freshly fallen snow. The dreamer awakens.

The structure of the dream, in 2-dimensional space, is the quartered mandala. In accordance with the above criteria, dream symbol location can be identified in terms of its off-centeredness and direction relative to one of the implied quadrants. The NW wooded area of the dream has, for the dreamer, an association with cross-country skiing. The first image further suggested by association is one of the skier dressed in the latest color-coordinated ski fashion. The image is Persona, and it dwells in the NW of the dream. Flowers grow inappropriately in the snow. But the flowers, symbol of the feminine, grow in the SW of the dreamscape, the appropriate dwelling place of the

Anima.

Ash cans line the SE quadrant. The dreamer's association is with father. He used to remove cans of ashes from a family coal stove. One of father's shadow characteristics was that he was alternatively and abruptly warm and cold, like fire and coal ash. With cross-dream consistency, Shadow is referred to in the SE quadrant. The NE is the realm of spirituality. Dreamer associations suggest that the house of the dreamscape's NE belongs to a woman. It is not clear, however, as to whether the home belongs to a wise woman -- an ancient witch, if you will, or to a destructive woman -- the modern re-conceptualization of the witch.

The NE and SE quadrants show 3-dimensionality. Smoke that spirals up from the house chimney, makes archetypal reference to spirit --smoke is that which is ephemeral and that which the wind (spiritus in Latin) takes. Spiritual individuation activity is suggested. In contradictory, and perhaps dialectic fashion, the silo towering phallus-like over the house means, for the dreamer, the presence of a great patriarchal God. In the SE, the ash cans evoke the collective unconscious. One ash can has a shiny metallic ring. The combined images of the ash and the ring amplify, for the dreamer, into memories from a reading years ago of the Nordic myth of the Ring of the Niebelungen, with its central symbols of the great World-Axis Ash Tree of the Father-God Wotan and his envied Ring of Rhine-Gold (Campbell, 1976).

What is the message of the dream for the individuation of the dreamer? This dream is part of a series -- a series, in fact, unified by images from the Niebelungen Myth. The series is dynamic in its presentation, over developmental time, of an individuation message. This dream ended and summarized the series by encapsulation of the whole in the part -- as a part of the hologram contains the whole. An explication of the dynamic aspect of this dream helps clarify dream analysis relative to individuation transformational processes.

The key to the dynamics of the dream is found in the figure transcribed in the snow on the driveway, made by the car's U-turn. The figure looks like a collapsed square -- a square made up of four inwardly bent, concave sides. When the dreamer awakened and drew the figure, he understood, in a flash of insight, the meaning of the figure and, consequently, the meaning of the dream for individuation. Before going to bed that night, the dreamer had re-read the end of Dante's <u>Divine Comedy</u> (Alighieri, 1947). The last stanzas provide a grand conclusion to the work and, at the same time, open a paradox of a puzzle:

> Like a geometer wholly dedicated
>   to squaring the circle, but who cannot find,
>   think as he may, the principle indicated --
>
> so did I study the supernatural face.
>   I yearned to know just how our image merges
>   into that circle, and how it there finds place;
>
> but mine were not the wings for such a flight.
>   Yet, as I wished, the truth I wished for came
>   cleaving my mind in a great flash of light.
>
> Here my powers rest from their high fantasy,
>   but already I could feel my being turned --
>   instinct and intellect balanced equally
>
> as in a wheel whose motion nothing jars --
>   by the Love that moves the Sun and the other stars. (pp.543-544)

Dante's reference to the great obsessive medieval quest -- to square the circle-- is a reference to geometry not to mathematics. The solution must take the form of geometric manipulations not numeric manipulations. The dreamer went to sleep wondering how a circle could be transformed into a square by means of cutting up a circle into pieces and rearranging it into a square. The problem is as maddening as Dante suggests. It is akin to the alchemist's quest for a transformational process which would convert base elements into gold. Like the transformational processes of alchemy, the underlying unconscious and archetypal meaning of the circle-to-square transformation is the quest for wholeness. No solution came to mind -- not to conscious mind: The dream, however, provided a solution.

Upon awakening, the dreamer was moved to draw on paper and cut out a figure representing abstractly the structure of the dream: the quartered circle, and then to cut the quartered circle into the four pie-shaped wedges it defined. What should be done next seemed apparent. He moved the four pieces of the circle, curved side first, into the configuration suggested by the shape in the snow of the drive-way: the figure with four concave sides. When the curved sides of the four wedges were placed in this pattern, i.e., when the four curved sides were configured to face each other and touch at their endpoints with no area of overlap, the total entity which resulted was a perfect square. The dream had instructed the dreamer to transform a circle into a square! That the key was a figure made by a broken-U indicated a deeper message of the dream. The dreamer had seen the phrase broken-U spelled in his mind as "broken-You." The dream was, consequently, about broken Self and its potential transformation to wholeness. (In terms of the criteria of Dante's day, the geometric solution the dream devised contained a flaw. In the nature of the flaw, however, was contained still another message about individuation. But that is for later elaboration.)

In most general terms, the dream helped the dreamer confront and make a decision about a matter of recent conscious concern. The dream landscape is not a reference to a place in reality. Each element in the landscape has a personal association with no necessary reference to normative cultural associations. Entering the farm house symbolized continuing an activity (unrelated to the literal activity of the dream). The dreamer was not sure if the activity would foster spiritual growth or be detrimental to it. The double witch associations state the ambiguity of the situation. The silo/phallus, however, seems to decide the issue. The dreamer's associations with the silo are to the evils of patriarchy. The activity the farmhouse symbolizes, therefore, is to be avoided. The Anima, Persona and Shadow/Father elements all reinforce for this dreamer the precise meaning of the conflict. The reader will not be bored with these details. The concern here is with a general explication of dream dynamics. Initially, the car is traveling East -- in a direction contrary to normal development, away from the setting sun, away from the traditional resting place of the soul, away from the West. The decision is made. The house is not entered. The car is turned around. If the message of the dream is heeded, there will be beneficial consequences for the dreamer. His car can now proceed on course to the West and his soul's destination.

The dream described above has been illustrative of dream statics and dynamics. It implies, by means of inductive logic, a set of procedures for dream analysis. A formal statement of dream analysis procedures follows next. The statement of procedures summarizes this section of the manuscript on dreams and sets the stage for the next section on art and unconscious expression.

Dream Analysis Procedures. -- In essence, one does dream analysis -- of one's own dreams or of an other's -- by examining the manifest content of dreams relative to their archetypal structure of form, plot, character and Self. The purpose of dream analysis is to uncover the complex which is dominating recent unconscious and conscious thoughts, feelings and actions and receive the message of the dream or dream series for conscious compensatory behavior. Dream analysis procedures are presented here as healing art (Mattoon, 1978).

The following statement of dream analysis procedures represents an integration of elements from Jung, Freud and personal experience-based inductive theory development. First, examine the manifest content of the dream relative to time, place, characters and plot. Make note of the decisive event or turning point of the dream.

Second, interpret the latent content of the dream. Begin by free association with key elements. For elements which cause resistance to free association, amplify relative to mythological or fairy tale references. One need not be a mythology expert to amplify. Consider the novels, movies or TV shows that the dreamer has enjoyed in particular or which have been re-read or viewed more than once. References to favorite stories are references to archetypal plot which echo great mythology. Amplification and association lead to the complex. Consequently, place the dream's latent content in the context of the last two three days. Also place the dream in the context of the recent dream series. The recurring symbols and motifs of the last two to one hundred dreams identify the complex.

Third, equate the dream characters to the Anima(us), Shadow, Persona and Ego splinter selves of the dreamer's Self. Assume that all the characters of the dream, whether they are recognized as people from waking life or not, as manifestations of different aspects of the dreamer. Examine the splinter selves in terms of their thoughts, feelings and actions relative to the complex; that is, consider the behavior of the splinter selves as messages for conscious behavior in terms of compensatory functioning relative to the complex.

Fourth, articulate the message, for the dreamer's dealing with the complex, as a hypothesis for further consideration by both the dreamer and the analyst. To proceed to further analysis, the analyst must receive verification of the hypothesis from the dreamer.

the message should resonate within the dreamer and seem insightful. The dreamer's rejection of the hypothesized message of the dream should not be construed as resistance.

Fifth and finally, diagram the archetypal structure of the dream in terms of the of the circle quadrants structure, and three-dimensional aspects, outlined above. Begin by drawing a circle within the square confines of a piece of paper. The practice can lead to transpersonal insights. Edinger (1972) informs us that, in Eastern symbolism, the square represents the earth as the person's domain and the circle represents God: "Thus when the dreamer draws a circle within the square... he is combining the individual and the personal with the eternal and transpersonal". (p. 211) Geometric drawing, therefore, enables visual verification and refinements of the analysis and healing message.

Art and other forms of creative projection, including literary and poetic expression, can be viewed as integral aspects of post-modernist understandings of the unconscious. Segal (1995) has argued that, as primitive and ancient cultures came to understand the unconscious by means of nature-oriented and religious projections and apprehensions; and as modern culture, in its proclamation that God is dead, came to be alienated from the unconscious and Self; our post-modernist (modernist-reactive) culture has reverted to projective -- but non-religious projective -- understandings of the unconscious. The art of Leonardo Da Vinci, and other artists, has been given psychoanalytic scrutiny, in terms of implied mandala design and expressions of differentiation of splinter selves (Neuman, 1974). The analyst Neuman has said that "every [art] symbol also expresses an essential unknown component of the psyche... ." (pp. 91-92). Given this precedent, and understanding of art as unconscious projection and apprehension, the original mandala aspect of dream analysis, presented in this work, opens the way to generalized healing applications of all forms of creative imagination, including art expression. After all, analysts have argued that all we know about the world comes through images (Hillman, 1976, p.118).

Generalized Analysis Procedures. -- In her work on the natural artistry of dreams, Mellick (1996) has noted: "not all insights are verbal. We do not need a cognitive, coherent, verbal presentation of dream wisdom for it to work its healing. So moving from one medium to another is also crucial to free-flowing creative dream work. For example, by translating the image and feeling of the dream... into an abstracted visual form... the dream transforms through different sense channels, giving us several opportunities to non-verbally absorb the experience." (pp.59-60) Mellick goes on to suggest that one draw one's most important dreams as mandalas, even specifying that a containing circle be drawn, divided into four quarters. (p. 203). The result is to be felt, however, and no principles of analysis are formulated. The case can be made that with minor and logical modifications, the same set of dream analysis procedures articulated above can be applied to the analysis of mandala art -- and can be used, as well, to structure Tarot readings (Nichols, 1980), other forms of creative imagination. Its application to mandala art has been the most direct and most intriguing.

In personal and student exercises, each individual has been asked to draw her or his dream. The dream may be the last one the person has had, the most memorable one or a recurring dream. One restriction is place on the drawing: students are asked to draw a large circle and work within the circle. They are encouraged to give free expression to their images and not feel self-conscious about their artistic abilities. In one variation of the exercise, students are asked to quarter the circle. Amazingly, the variation's restriction has proven to be unnecessary. In personal content analysis research, students not instructed to quarter the circle do so anyway, in terms of the implicit placement of dream images within a quadrant structure. Content analysis of quadrant imagery further reveals that latent content interpretation of each of the four quadrants is best guided by the splinter selves quadrant theory outlined above, i.e., the SW, SE, NW and NE quadrants contains expression, respectively, of Anima(us), Shadow, Persona and Ego!

Dream analysis application to mandala art has invaluable implications for defining not only a spiritually-based practice, but also a diversity-based practice. Mandala art is a product of diverse world cultures, from the Tibetan to the indigenous cultures of the Americas. For example, illustrative of spiritual healing practice among the indigenous peoples of the American South West is the use of the Medicine Wheel. In Jungian terms, it is used for self-insight and self-transformation to wholeness. These cultures bring special insight and application to the use of the quartered circle for healing. This section of the manuscript concludes with an exploration of the concept of spirituality itself, as spirituality is infused within and throughout all topics under the rubric of healing art practice.

SPIRITUALITY

Synchronicty

Introduction. -- <u>Flatland</u> is a novel written over a century ago (1983/1884). Originally, its Swiftian adventure plot may have caught the interest of science-fiction lovers, but more recently physicists interested in finding the metaphors to express non-mathematically the hard science of time-space relativity have found a treasure of heuristic ideas in this book. The perspective that this work fosters helps one develop a conceptual break-through relative to time and, in doing so, helps introduce a key concept for understanding the theoretical underpinning of spirituality: the concept of transcendence. Following an exploration of time-transcendent, linkage will be made to the other central concept of spirituality theory: meaning. Together, these understandings will allow application to principles of spiritually-based practice -- from individual healing to spiritually-rooted social justice.

Time Transcendent. -- We take for granted the realities of our three-dimensional world. Three dimensions define reality. We need not turn to theology, however, to try to understand the transcendent reality beyond our perception. Hard science will do. Physics tells us of the reality of the fourth dimension -- the temporal dimension of space. We need not master the mathematics of relativity to master this understanding. The right brain is as insightful as the left. We learn as profoundly by means of metaphor as we do by math. Physicist Capra (1976) has said, in his study of the Tao of physics, that we need "a dynamic interplay between mystical intuition and scientific analysis... our attitude is too young...too rational, male, and aggressive." (p.297). Let us try, therefore, to understand how reality is perceived by creatures who live in a two-dimensional world -- the plane of Flatland. That should not be too difficult for three-dimensional creatures. The greater question will become: can we then by means of this extended metaphor understand what are the realities of the four-dimensional world beyond us?

Imagine our three-dimensional existence as life in a box, i.e., a cube. We are free to travel left and right (along the x-axis of the cube), back and forth (the z-axis) as well as up and down (the y-axis). Imagine the world of the people of Flatland. They dwell on the plane that is, say, the base of the box. They can experience left-right movement (x-axis) and back-forth movement (z-axis), but not up-down movement (y-axis). And what they cannot experience they cannot conceive -- at least not without a little help from us three-dimensional creatures.

We visit their plane and speak to the Flatlanders from our transcendent realm. We ask them to conceive of a 10-inch line. They have no trouble with that, they can draw it. We ask them to conceive a 10-inch square. That too can be drawn. We then ask them to conceive a 10-inch cube. Now, we sense a problem developing. The mathematicians among them reason that if the line can be represented by the number 10 and the square can be represented by the square of 10, i.e., 100; then the cube can be represented by the cube of 10, i.e., 1000. How would we help them, however, reach understanding beyond the mathematical abstractions and "see" the third dimension? Helping them to grasp the idea of 2-dimensional objects in motion -- motion in an up-down dimension may be the key.

We may try asking the Flatlanders to study the square they draw in their plane and try to conceive a similar square "out there" in another plane of existence, i.e., "up there." When they have mastered that, we ask them to apply their familiar concept of motion; however, motion will not be defined as left-right nor back-forth. We ask the Flatlanders to move, conceptually, their real square from their "here" to their "out there": -- until the two squares touch. (The movement is along what we would call the y-axis or up-down dimension of reality.) Move the real square back here, we'll say, then move it back "up." Keep it in motion, we'll add. What is the "cube"? -- they may ask: Is it the square here or the square out there? You're forgetting the factor of motion, we'll respond. The cube is neither the square here nor the one up there; rather, it is that structure defined by the motion of the square itself. By this means, we help the Flatlanders conceive the mystery of the cube -- a mystery for their two-dimensional minds, a reality as we three-dimensional creatures can truly know it.

If cube is a reality, should the Flatlanders not sense it or intuit it in some way, even in their two-dimensional world? They do intuit motion in the third dimension of space, they define it as time! To understand how they re-define motion in the third dimension of space as time, let us try to conceive how the Flatlanders would interpret the visit to their 2-dimensional plane of the 3-dimensional entity we call "sphere."

Sphere descends into their plane downward along the y-axis of the reality of the encompassing 3-dimensional cube. Sphere enters the plane fully, stopping at the point of its widest diameter (its equator, if you will). What do the Flatlanders perceive? They cannot see beyond their 2-dimensional world, so they do not see a sphere. They can see, however, that portion of the sphere which intersects with their flat plane of existence. They perceive a circle. It is a mystery to them how the circle appeared, but it is there and it is real, manifest in their world. Imagine that the sphere moves on down our y-axis and disappears from Flatland. Imagine that it returns again from on up high. This time, the Flatlanders are ready to report what they see. First they see a dot on their plane. The dot gradually expands into a wider and wider circle until it seems to reach its fullest form and then grows smaller and smaller until the circle is again a dot and again it disappears.

The social worker among the Flatlanders, well versed in developmental psychology, does not report what she sees quite in the geometrical way described above. The social worker tells us that today a circle was born and later died. Its was born as a cute little dot; it grew as it developed into a full circle; it withered as it aged and shrank again into a dot; and finally it died. Developmental concepts such as birth and growth and aging and death are temporal concepts. To make sense of the visit of the sphere to their world, the Flatlanders not only reduced sphere to circle, they reduced physical motion in a real dimension of space to a conceptualization of time. Time, for them, is motion in the third dimension. Time is a real dimension of space. It is y-axis space/motion. We 3-dimensional creatures know that. Flatlanders cannot know time as a dimension of space. They must intuit it as the abstraction -- real to them in their social/cultural construction of reality -- that they call, and we call, time.

Of our misperception of the spacial reality of time, a science-writer and <u>Flatland</u> fan (Garnett, 1983) has argued: "If there is motion of our 3-dimensional space relative to the 4th dimension, all the changes we experience and assign the flow of time will be simply due to this movement, the whole of the future as well as the past always existing in the fourth dimension" (p. xviii). This statement of time/space relativity is easier to comprehend given the analogy and set of metaphors provided by Flatland. It helps us make sense of the theological, as well as physics-related, notion that to a divine omniscience past, present and future are one. Take again the perspective of the sphere. Say, after it passes down through Flatland's plane, that it overhears the Flatlanders' bemoaning the poor sphere's death. "I'm right here below you," says the sphere, but its message from the third dimension is lost in the 2-dimensional world.

What the sphere knows as above, plane-level and below, the Flatlanders can intuit only as past present and future. The Flatlanders' past is gone forever as they await the future in the present moment. The sphere's past is now. It is a dimension of vertical space. The sphere can traverse past, present and future and back again as readily as it can affect motion up and down in the third dimension. For the sphere, time is the oneness of the y-axis of space. For the sphere, there is no causal flow of time from past to future. Future can flow into present and present into past.

The Flatlanders' sense of time can be understood by sphere in acausal context. How can we 3-dimensional creatures understand our sense of time in acausal context? We 3-dimensional creatures understand the fourth dimension of space as temporal flow. We re-construct movement within the fourth dimension of space, for our socio-cultural reality, as time flow. This has implications for our understanding of causal connections within reality. The future, we say, cannot cause the past or present. Yet, small-particle quantum mechanics physicists do note the influence of "future" particalization on "present" particle materialization. A formula describing an electron, for example, is read simultaneously as a formula describing a positron moving backwards in time (Feynman,

1985, pp.95-98). The physicist's mathematical conceptualization, however, derives from relativity theory and accepts the fourth dimension as a spacial reality different from the layperson's culturally-laden conceptualization of time. The lay person does intuit these truths. Synchronicity and spirituality are the contextual terms that most often make sense to us 3-dimensional creatures.

Implications of Time-transcendent for Spirituality and Synchronicity. -- Consider the implications for our spiritual understanding by again trying to understand the relationship between the Flatlanders' and the sphere's realities. The Flatlanders bemoan the loss of sphere because it is gone from existence. Sphere has died. But sphere is puzzled by this understanding. Sphere knows it exists. It has not died. It continues to exists in the third dimension. The Flatlanders do not understand that sphere has merely moved out of time -- Flatlanders' time.

How has our limited, socially constructed notion of time limited our understanding of death? Are those who have died in our 3-dimensional world gone? Do the dead cease to exist, or are they merely removed from our illusion of time? Are our ancestors frustrated in their attempts to be heard in our world? When they speak from the fourth dimension, do we fail to hear? Is it merely their bodies which are gone? Do their souls, and our souls, remain eternal in the timelessness of the fourth dimension? Is sphere to circle as soul is to body? Time-transcendent is the element of transcendence in spirituality. And in the powerful re-conceptualization death and life which it allows -- in its challenge to our socially constructed understanding of death, time-transcendent is also the element of meaning in spirituality.

What then is synchronicity? It has been referred to by Jung (1973) as a principle of acausality. Jung (1971) defines synchronicity as, "a meaningful coincidence of two or more events, when something other than the probability of chance is involved." (p.505) The "meaningfulness" of the coincidence is imparted by the individual witnessing and interpreting the events. The word "coincidence" persists as an element in synchronicity's popular definition because of our cultures' general understanding of causality. Our 3-dimensional world understanding of causality includes the notions that future cannot cause present and that one event cannot cause another event distant from it in time and space. Yet we marvel at the meaningfulness of events which cannot have been brought about by their apparent causes -- and label them "coincidence." Jung's thoughts on synchronicity were influenced by his work and discussions with physicist Wolfgang Pauli (Wolf, 1994). Quantum physics, like the Tao, posits a dynamic unity underlying the perceived dualities of reality.

Jung's conception of synchronicity is more Taoist than the popular (Rosen, 1996). Concepts of causality and coincidence need play no role. Jung (1971) has described the case of a patient of his who was resistant to understanding the deeper meaning of the symbols of her dreams. From session to session she would remain concrete in her interpretations of dream elements. During a break-through session, the woman spoke of having dreamt of a golden scarab. During her telling of the dream, something tapped on the office window. Jung turned and went to the window. He saw a scarabaeid beetle whose gold-green color gives it resemblance to a golden scarab. He handed the beetle to his patient and told her that this was her scarab. The incident punctured the resistance of her over-intellectualization and treatment continued with more satisfactory results.

Jung never suggests that the woman's or his need for a break-through caused the beetle to appear. The world does not revolve around any one person. Jung's conception of the world is that all things and all events are interconnected. The interconnection of events transcends Western cultural notions of time and space. Event interconnections are simultaneous, and non-local as well as local. Event happenings fit the Eastern, Taoist conceptualization of the interconnectedness of all things. We need only drop the veil of Maya and learn to go with the flow and interconnectedness of all things in order to understand the meaning of synchronistic events. We have seen that for Jung the unconscious mind stands in compensatory relationship to the conscious mind in the oneness that is self. Now we see also that for Jung the Self itself stands in compensatory relationship to Nature. There are messages for our individuation and growth from within, from our dreams; as well as from without, from our synchronicity experiences.

Dreams of Prophesy. -- Jung has referred to the Collective Unconscious as timeless. The archetypes of the Collective Unconscious are universal and beyond limiting Western cultural conceptualizations of time and space. Jung (1989a) has said: "I have been convinced that at least part of our psychic existence is characterized by a relativity of space and time. This relativity seems to increase, in proportion to the distance from consciousness, to an absolute condition of timelessness and spacelessness." (p.305) The temporal dimension of the Collective Unconscious is time-transcendent. When one enters the unconscious world of the dream, does one have access to past and future in the present of the dream? Can the dream traverse the space of time, from past to future, as readily as the sphere of <u>Flatland</u> traverses up and down the time dimension of the Flatlanders?

Dreams of prophesy would suggest the reality of time-transcendent in the dream's realm of the unconscious. Wolf (1994) reports twelve formal experiments on dream telepathy and notes 9 show statistically significant results. Content analysis of personal dreams shows dreams of prophesy to be rare. Two seemed to have occurred over a 25-year period. (Both occurred in the same year.) The following example illustrates one of two personal dreams of prophesy. It has not been uncommon for the dreamer to experience death anniversary dreams. His father died on a December 1st. Like clockwork every year, a dream of father's death occurs after going to sleep on November 30th -- even when, as often happens, there is no conscious memory of the death anniversary. An unusual twist to this common type of phenomenon occurred once when the dreamer reviewed his dream log and noted a dream he had recorded about a dear colleague. The colleague, a religiously devout and deeply spiritual woman, was a spirit of the dead in the dream. She takes the dreamer to visit her tomb. They travel to a pyramid. The woman points to the pyramid (in the NE quadrant of the dream) and talks about her happiness in the afterlife, but also of the value of holding on to life as long as possible -- until one's purpose is served.

Although the dream was recorded not far back chronologically in his log, the dreamer could barely remember having written it. The dreamer noted the date of the recorded dream: September 16, 1991. Something about this date seemed very familiar and very unusual at the same time. He checked a secretary's calendar. Yes, this was a night-before death anniversary dream. His colleague had died on a September 17th. The astounding fact, however, was that she had died on September 17, 1992. This was the only dream in the dreamer's log ever recorded about her. It had the characteristics of his death anniversary dreams of others. And this was, in fact, by date, a death anniversary dream -- one, however, which occurred on the anniversary of his colleague's death one year prior to her death. Neither his colleague nor her doctor knew one year prior to her death that she was ill or in any danger of contracting a terminal disease. This news came nine months prior to her death.

Coincidence? Quite possibly. This dreamer has recorded many dreams each year for almost twenty-five years. That a couple of those dreams would seem prophetic in retrospect is possible, if not probable. Nevertheless, the dreamer had a synchronistic sense about this dream. At the time this coincidence was noted, the dreamer was planning a trip to Sicily. It was to be followed by a trip to Egypt and the pyramids. On the assumption that there was more to the dream than coincidence, the dreamer chose to heed his interpretation of one of the dream's messages. He went to the pyramids first and later followed the Egyptian tour up with his long-desired trip to Sicily. While in Egypt, he learned of an incident in Sicily which resulted in the deaths of a group of tourists. Later, when he did come to tour Sicily safely, during the time period originally planned for Egypt, he and the world learned of the first murderous attack upon tourists in Egypt.

The dream could not be construed as a warning from a concerned spirit -- his beloved colleague was not dead at the time of the dream. On the other hand, it was not his colleague who gave the warning; it was an archetypal figure from the Collective Unconscious -- the timeless unconscious, in which future can influence present, and in which past, present and future are one. Synchronicity is never merely about coincidence. It is about meaningful coincidence. And it is the individual, influenced by his or her sensitivities, intuitive "reasoning" and spiritual outlook, who invests meaning.

The Uses of Acausality in Everyday Life. -- As noted earlier, principles of dream analysis can be applied to the study of mandalas of personal expression. These principles apply as well to Tarot readings -- in which the Tarot spread is configured to represent the four-part mandala structure of the unconscious. Consequently, unconscious projections to the archetypal card characters may be analyzed in conformity to the principles of dream quadrant analysis described above. And to both practice activities, as well as to all exercises of creative imagination, may be applied a sensitivity to synchronistic happenings.

Content analyses of Tarot spread readings and personal mandala expressions indicate not only a consistency with principles of quadrant structure dream analysis, but also with prophetic dreams. It is the NE quadrant of the Tarot spread and the NE quadrant of mandala, as it is the NE quadrant of the prophetic dream, which looks to the future. The wholeness of the mandala evolves, as does spiritual growth and self-transformation. The Goddess Kundalini, who guides the practice of spiritual transformation, rises through chakras, illustrated in ancient drawings as mandalas (Pretat, 1994). With a spiritual sensitivity to the synchronistic events of everyday life, fostered by techniques of creative imagination, transcendent messages for meaning in life and self-transformation can be found in one's natural surroundings. And does not Jung state that Nature stands in compensatory relationship to us individuating beings?

A Working Definition of Spirituality

Spiritually-based Practice. -- Spirituality is an orientation to life and death. Beyond this statement, there may be little agreement among scholars and practitioners as to what is spirituality. "Transcendence" and "meaning-in-life" are almost universally used concepts in the spirituality literature, and this work's theoretical orientation keeps them central. Spirituality is seen as an aspect of development. Individuation may be interpreted, from a spiritual perspective, as development informed by a sense of the transcendence of life in the search for meaning within the continuum of life and death.

For social gerontology, the theoretical orientation of this work strongly suggests the need for a spirituality-oriented revisiting of Disengagement Theory. Important work along this line has been begun by Tornstam's introduction of the notion of Gero-transcendence (1989). Tornstam postulates an aging shift from the materialistic and rational to the cosmic and transcendent. More recently, Schoots (1995) has called for the study of critical life points for an understanding of these types of moral and spiritual shifts and the directions they may take.

For social work, one of the first defining works to appear on the topic of spirituality, an article by Dudley and Helfont (1990), offers a definition of the spiritual dimension "as encompassing the need to find satisfactory answers to the meaning of life, illness, and death, as well as seeking a deeper relationship with God, others and self." (p.287) This may be seen as one useful working definition of spirituality for social work -- with the addition of certain friendly amendments. Given this work's emphasis on secular social work practice applications, spirituality need be viewed, at least in part, in ways distinct from religion. The term "God" in the above definition may serve to further the confusion between spirituality and religion and, therefore, may best be replaced with a more general term such as "transcendent power." The term "illness" should be viewed, from the multidisciplinary point of view characteristic of social work, as encompassing all suffering and, consequently, the idea underlying "illness" would be better communicated by the word "suffering."

For social work, the definition's phrase about seeking a deeper relationship with others and self is particularly relevant. Each individual in the helping professions is admonished to "know thyself." Paradoxically, it may be argued that to search inward for a sense of self deeper than the social self --beyond the definitions of self which derive from the social roles, statuses and identities of Persona -- is, ultimately, to more meaningfully connect with others. To be able to see and respect one's own core humanity as an innate basis of self-worth, is to be able to appreciate and respect the human dignity of others independent of their social statuses. Such spiritual social wisdom may be the basis for compassion -- an attitude toward others which seems to pervade all formal expressions of spirituality. And is compassion not a social form of transcendence in which one gives of self in a manner which protects the giving up of self? (The giving of self is not to be confused with the giving up of self. The latter may have more to do with self-destructive dependence than with the self-enhancing spirituality of compassion.)

Compassion is, in fact, at the heart of a definition of spirituality in social work offered by Canda (1988): It involves a sense of meaning through "moral relations" with others and "moral relations" is suggested to necessarily imply compassion toward others as an outcome of authentic communion in relationships. The following quote, cited by Kilpatrick and Holland (1990), of Frankel, states well the relationship between the transcendence aspect of spirituality and compassion:

> "Being human is always directed...to a meaning to fulfill or another human being to encounter, a cause to serve or a person to love. ...not by concerning himself with his self's actualization, but by forgetting himself, overlooking himself and focusing outward... What is called self-actualization is and must retain the unintended effect of self-transcendence. (p.135)

Seeing spirituality as associated with a meaningful sense of Self, apart from socially defined meanings of self, helps crystallize the key distinction between spirituality and religion. Religion is another form of social institution. It is another social agent for the granting of roles, statuses, beliefs, values and practices defined as socially meaningful. As does school, work, and family, religion provides merely another social identity -- an identity which by definition cannot be transcendent of social meaning but rooted in it.

Rooted in social meaning, the religious sense of self is as fragile as any other social self. One can view the work of social work practice crisis intervention as having to help people cope with the insults to sense of self derived from social role identity loss, i.e., as insults to Persona. For example, consider some of the presenting problem foci of some of the typical advanced practice concentrations of social work. In Family Mental Health curriculum, social workers learn to help clients cope with the pain of divorce, i.e., self-identity diminishment due to social role loss; in Occupational Social Work, they learn to help workers deal with job loss or demotion, i.e., self-identity diminishment due to social role loss; and in Gerontology, they learn to help the elderly cope with widowhood, the empty nest syndrome and retirement, i.e., self-identity diminishment due to social role loss. Many of the crises of social work are spiritual crises. With a strong sense of Self not contingent upon social statuses and roles, clients would be better able to cope with the practical problems of role loss. Spirituality-based social work, in helping to impart a spiritual --socially transcendent -- sense of Self, can empower its clients in their attempts to establish an inherently meaningful life style.

The orientation of this work to theory, spirituality and practice, therefore, facilitates the development of a practice which fosters spiritual consciousness. The guiding principle, and working definition of spiritual consciousness, for such a practice is offered to be the following: ***Spiritual Consciousness is an orientation to life and death characterized by the individual's search for meaning transcendent of socially constructed reality***. Given social work's community service values, as well as individual service values, this guiding principle must lead to the establishment of spiritual community as well as to individual healing. Consciousness is emergent from community. Correspondingly, social workers who can appreciate the humanity of the individual in a way not contingent upon social status and role-identity values are in a position to empower both themselves and their clients to work to eliminate social oppression. A society free of oppression is a spiritual community, of collective spiritual consciousness, whose members are truly free to grow to their full spiritual potential in their living lives of transcendent meaning.

Personal Transformation and Spiritual Community. -- Spiritually-based practice in social work has placed its greatest emphasis on therapeutic intervention (Borenzweig, 1984). This work attempts an expansion of the concept of practice which fosters spiritual consciousness to the community level. Personal and social transformation are viewed as linked. Neuman (1974) has said that "the knowledge that man undergoes transformations, and that the world transforms itself with and for him, is an element of every human culture." (p.154) Central to the integrated person/society model of spiritually-based practice will be the meaning imparted by the structural metaphor of the quartered circle as Self as well as the dynamics of the individuation process.

The quartered circle of splinter selves -- Ego, Persona, Anima(us) and Shadow -- transforms into the whole circle of Self, as Ego consciously and dialectically incorporates the powerful archetypal forces of Persona, Anima(us) and Shadow. The first step in personal transformation to spiritual consciousness is Persona deflation -- that process which leads to recognition of the superficiality of meaning associated with socially constructed status and role realities. To survive in the world, one need wear and act through the social masks one is required to use. To over identify with the masks and come to see them as true Self, is to lose one's soul. To see the masks as socially constructed facades, is to transcend Persona identity and embrace the sense of meaning-in-life which derives from knowing true Self. The next transformational steps of individuation are those which end one's projections of Anima(us) and Shadow. Differentiation gives way to the integration which is individuation. Genuine relationship becomes possible as splinter selves are given conscious expression.

To own Shadow is not to bring evil forward. To know Anima is not to become effeminate. The process of individuation is compensatory and the resulting wholeness of Self is dialectic. During de-differentiation, Shadow aggression encounters its conscious compensatory aspect of passive acceptance of exploitation of self. The result for transformed Self is neither aggression nor passivity but dialectic assertiveness. Likewise, the archetypal characteristic of Independent Woman or Gentleman emerges dialectically from the encountering of Animus' Nag with consciousness' compensatory Compliant Woman, or Anima's Wimp with consciousness' He-man. As does the Yin-Yang, the quartered circle spins and, in its motion, dissolves it quadripartite structure into a dynamic circular form of wholeness. This metaphor is in keeping with the ancient Chinese distinction between t'ai chi -- Yin-Yang circle, dichotomized and with circles of "the other" in each half, and wu chi -- the empty circle of the time before opposites (Neumann, 1995, pp. 8,12).

In the dream about individuation described earlier, one in which a circle was transformed into a square, something seemed wrong to the dreamer. Part of the concern was left-brained, in that it is well known that a precise solution to the squaring of the circle is mathematically impossible: the solution necessarily involves measurement using Pi which, as an irrational number, allows no line- or plane-related finite cutting point (Dunham, 1990). The right-brained concern was more pressing: The dream's metaphorical message for individuation seemed off. After all, although the dream showed how a circle could be transformed into a square, it did not meet Dante's culture's exacting requirement that the square be of the same area as the circle. Another dream, which followed this one in series -- a dream about rounding a baseball diamond's bases -- told that the first dream got the metaphor backwards. The direction of individuation is not from circle to square, but from square to circle. One does not move from whole Self to four-sided splinter selves; one transforms from splinter self-quarters to centered wholeness. Differentiation of splinter selves is not the end of the individuation process. It is the Yang to the Yin of de-differentiation. The individuated soul emerges dialectically. T'ai chi becomes wu chi.

Spiritual Community. -- For deflated Persona, Anima(us) expression and Shadow manifestation to be accepted, social supports are necessary. No individuated person is an island. As described earlier in this work, wholeness of Self emerges dialectically in relationships. Spiritual meaning transcends socially constructed reality and is born in genuine relationships which allow each individual full expression of whole Self. The spiritual journey to wholeness necessarily involves the search for spiritual community. The notion of spiritual community is not to be confused with the extremist sect. When the individual is forced to surrender control to social organization, the community is necessarily oppressive (Laudry, 1995). The spiritual community is one free of oppression and one compassionate in each member's treatment and acceptance of the Self of every other individual. In community practice which fosters spiritual consciousness, spirituality is not solely private expression. Individual wholeness emerges from a dialectic of Self and social transformation – a dialectic which signals the birth of spiritual consciousness.

Social work community practice involves recognition and celebration of the contributions of People of Color and women. The African American Church (Sanders, 1996; Hawkins, 1997), Latino (Baez, 1996) and other religious ethnic congregations (Kung, 1990), Gay and Lesbian (Cuthbertson, 1996) and Feminist networks (Mellick, 1996) constitute spiritual communities. Indigenous peoples, have long maintained communities of special spiritual insights and support of unconscious Self-expressions. All of American society can learn from its indigenous peoples and be hastened in its spiritual transformation -- and perhaps be re-born to its original nature-oriented form. Navarro (1997) reports that of the Native students he worked with, oppressed by main-stream culture and struggling with substance abuse, many were helped by their construction and use of a Medicine Wheel. Jung (1989a) has reported that he achieved greater insights as he learned from the Pueblo Indians. (p.246)

Individual and community stand in compensatory relationship. Practice which fosters spiritual consciousness, therefore, is community practice and, by means of it, social work can be the dialectic force for individual spiritual transformation.

REFERENCES

Abbott, E.A. (1983) <u>Flatland</u>. New York: Harper Perennial. (original work published 1884)

Alighieri, D. (1947). <u>The divine comedy.</u> (L. Binyon, Trans.). In P. Milano (Ed.), <u>The portable Dante</u> (pp.3-544). New York: The Viking Press. (original works published Fourteenth Century)

Aziz, R. (1990). <u>C.G. Jung's psychology of religion and synchronicity</u>. Albany: State University of New York Press.

Baez, E. (1996). Spirituality and the gay Latino client. <u>Human Services for Gay People</u>, pp.69-81.

Bickerton, D. (1990). <u>Language and species</u>. Illinois: University of Chicago Press.

Blakeslee, S. (1991, January 15). The brain can 'see' what eyes cannot. <u>The New York Times</u>, pp.c1, c8.

Blakeslee, S. (1992a, October 27). Nerve cell rhythm may be key to consciousness. <u>The New York Times</u>, pp.c1, c8.

Blakeslee, S. (1992b, January 7). Scientists unraveling chemistry of dreams. <u>The New York Times</u>, pp.c1, c10.

Bopp, J. et al. (1989). <u>The sacred tree: Reflections on Native American spirituality</u>. Wisconsin: Lotus Light.

Borenzweig, H. (1984). Jung and social work. Lanham, Maryland: University Press of

America.

Campbell, J. (1976). The masks of God: Occidental Mythology. New York: Penguin Books. (original work published 1964)

Campbell, J. (1976). The masks of God: Primitive Mythology. New York: Penguin Books. (original work published 1959)

Canda, E. R. (1988). Conceptualizing spirituality for social work: Insights from diverse perspectives. Social Thought, 14(1), pp.30-46.

Capra, F. (1976) The Tao of physics. New York: Bantam Books.

Coleman, D. (1988, May 24) Personal myths bring cohesion to the chaos of each life. The New York Times, pp. c1, c11.

Coleman, D. (1992, June 23) Your unconscious mind may be smarter than you. The New York Times, pp. c, c11.

Cornell, J. (1994). Mandala: Luminous symbols for healing. Illinois: Quest Books.

Cuthbertson, K.L. (1996). Coming out/conversion: An exploration of gay religious experience. The Journal of Men's Studies, 4, (3), p.193.

Dudley, J.R. & Helfgott, C. (1990). Exploring a place for spirituality in the social work curriculum. Journal of Social Work Education, 26(3), pp.287-294.

Dunham, W. (1990). Journey through genius. New York: John Wiley and Sons.

Edinger, E.F. Ego and archetype. Boston: Shambala Publications, 1972.

Feynman, R.P. (1985). QED. New Jersey: Princeton University Press.

Freud, S. (1965). The interpretation of dreams. (J. Stachey, Trans.) New York: Avon Books. (original work published 1900)

Garnett, W. (1983) Introduction. In E.A. Abbott, Flatland (pp. xv-xviii). New York: Harper Perennial.

Gergen, K. (1971) The concept of self. New York: Holt, Rinehart and Winston.

Hatab, L.J. (1990). Myth and personality. Illinois: Open Court Publishing.

Hawkins, D. (1997, October 16). In the spirit of healing. Black Issues in Higher Education, p.36.

Hill, G.S. (1992). Masculine and feminine: The natural flow of opposites in the psyche. Boston: Shambala.

Hillman, J. (1972). The myth of analysis. New York: Harper Perennial.

Hillman, J. (1976). Peaks and vales. In Needleman, J., & Lewis, D. (Eds.), On the way to self-knowledge (pp.114-147). New York: Alfred A. Knopf.

Jung, C.G. (1971). Aion: Phenomenology of the self. In J. Campbell (Ed.), The portable Jung (R.F.C. Hull, Trans.). (pp.139-162). New York: Penguin. (original work published 1954)

Jung, C.G. (1989a). Memories, dreams, reflections. (A. Jaffe, Trans.). New York: Vintage Books. (original work published 1961)

Jung, C.G. (1989b). Mysterium Coniunctionis. (R.F.C. Hall, Trans.). New Jersey: Princeton University Press. (original work published 1955)

Jung, C.G. (2009). The Red Book: Liber Novus (M. Kyburz, J. Peck and S. Shamdasani, Trans.). London and New York: Norton and Company.

Jung, C.G. (1973). Synchronicity: An acausal connecting principle (R.F.C. Hull, Trans.). New York: First Princeton/ Bollington Paperback Edition. (original work published 1960)

Kafatos, M. and Nadeau, R. (1990). The conscious universe. New York: Springer-Verlag.

Kilpatrick, A.C. & Holland, T.P. (1990). Spiritual dimensions of practice. The Clinical Supervisor, 8(2), pp.125-140.

Kung, C.H. (1990). Struggle to be the sun again: Introducing Asian women's theology. California: Orbis Books.

Laudry, J. (1995). Archetypal psychology and the twelve-step movement. In J. Hillman, et al. (Eds.), Disillusionment (pp.1-20). Woodstock, Connecticut: Spring Publications.

Mansfield, V. (1995). Synchronicity, science and soul making. Illinois: Open Court Publishing.

Mattoon, M.A. (1978) Applied dream analysis: A Jungian approach. Washington, D.C.: V.H. Winston and Sons.

Mellick, J. (1996). The natural artistry of dreams: Creative ways to bring the wisdom of dreams to waking life. Berkeley, California: Conari Press.

Moore, R. and Gillette, D. (1990) King, warrior, magician, lover. San Francisco: Harper

Colins Publisher.

Navarro, J. et al. (1997). Substance abuse and spirituality: A program for Native American students. American Journal of Health Behavior, 21 (1), pp.3-11.

Neumann, E. (1974). Art and the creative unconscious. (R. Manheim, Trans.). New Jersey: Princeton University Press. (original work published 1959).

Neumann, E. (1995) The origins and history of consciousness. (R.F.C. Hall, Trans.). Princeton, New Jersey: Bollingen Foundation. (original work published 1954)

Nichols, S. (1980). Jung and Tarot: An archetypal journey. Maine: Weiser, Inc.

Nietzsche, F. (1954). The birth of tragedy. (C.P. Fadiman, Trans.). In The philosophy of Nietzsche. (pp.947-1088). New York: Random House.

Pinker, S. (1994). The language instinct. New York: William Marrow and Company.

Plotinus. (1991). The enneads. (S. Mackenna, Trans.). London: Penguin Books. (original works published Third Century)

Pretat, J.R. (1994). Coming to age. Toronto: Inner City Books.

Robertson, Robin. (1995). Jungian archetypes. Maine: Nicolas-Hays.

Rosen, D. (1996) The Tao of Jung. New York: Viking Arkana.

Sanders, C.J. (1996). Saints in exile: The Holiness-Pentecostal experience in African American religion and culture. New York: Oxford University Press.

Schoots, J.J.F. (1995). Gerodynamics: Toward a branching theory of aging. Canadian Journal on Aging, 14, pp.74-81.

Segal, R.A. (1995). Jung's fascination with Gnosticism. In R.A. Segal (Ed.), The allure of Gnosticism (pp.26-38). Illinois: Open Court.

Singer, J. (1973). Boundaries of the soul. New York: Anchor Books.

Smith, C.D. (1990). Jung's quest for wholeness. Albany: State University of New York Press.

Stevens, A. (1991). The shadow in history and literature. In C. Zweig and J. Abrams (Eds.), Meeting the shadow (pp.27-28). Los Angeles: Jeremy P. Tarcher, Inc.

Tornstam, L. (1989). Gero-transcendence: A reformulation of the disengagement theory. Aging, 1, pp.55-63.

von Franz, M. (1998). On dreams and death. (E. Kennedy-Xipolitas, Trans.). Illinois: Open Court Publishing Company. (original work published 1984)

Wolf, F.A. (1994). The dreaming universe. New York: Touchstone.

DEDICATION

For my daughter Irena, who shared with me her highly perceptive insights into the Universal Archetypes to be found in post-modern and feminist literature.

Printed in Great Britain
by Amazon